Army Cadet Basic Training Handbook 2019/20 Edition

Knowle Farm Business Centre, Wadhurst Road,
Frant, Tunbridge Wells, Kent, TN3 9EJ
United Kingdom
www.one8e.co.uk • info@one8e.co.uk

ISBN: 978-0-9567790-8-3

Army Cadet: Basic Training Handbook
This volume: 2nd edition

Produced by one8e publishing
Published by one8e publishing

Printed by Fraser Allen

Items for photos on loan from www.cadetdirect.com
Photos taken at Cranbrook detachment, Kent ACF

Edited by Samantha Hazlewood
Internal photography by Mark Roe - Sports photographer
Cover photography by Jason Kemp
Cover design and layout by PSD Innovative

Contents

Book guide

This handbook is an unofficial reference guide for instructors, PIs and cadets. Every lesson from every subject is covered, along with all testing requirements. There is also an introduction to the Army Cadet Force, places to record detachment specific information and a lesson checklist.

Cadets

Cadets should keep this handbook on them at all times. It is designed to be able to fit into the pocket of combat trousers or combat jacket. Extra notes can be made within the book as lessons are taught, and can be referred to between parade nights to confirm what has been learnt. An adult instructor should sign the lesson checklist on the last page every time a lesson is given. The testing part of the book must be completed under the supervision of an adult instructor.

Instructors & PIs

Instructors are to use this as a reference guide only. The chapter header page for each subject outlines the number of lessons to be delivered as well as the overall aims. There is also a list of where the up to date source material can be found. This handbook does not replace the current manuals, but can be used as a handy reference tool when delivering lessons. Lesson plans should still be used to give structure and timings to lessons.

Due to the ever changing nature of the Army Cadet Force, it is wise to check the original source material listed on a regular basis.

The last chapter contains all testing information for every subject, these can be filled in and kept as evidence to enable cadets to sign off their basic training.

Certain tests given are not officially required, but we feel help to confirm understanding from cadets (these are noted on the individual test pages).

NOTE: Chapter Seven, Skill At Arms, provides revision only and should not be used for delivering lessons. SAA lessons should be taught from the official manuals by a current and competent SAA instructor.

Feedback

Although every effort has been made to make this publication as accurate as possible, there may be something we've missed. If you spot anything or have any suggestions, please email us so that we can improve future editions.

info@cadetbooks.com

Thanks for reading!

CHAPTER ONE

Aim

By the end of this chapter, you will understand the following:

- Who sponsors the Army Cadet Force
- Our link to the British Army
- What subjects you will study
- How you will progress as a cadet within the ACF
- What APC stands for
- Who to go to if you have a problem

What is the ACF?

- The ACF (Army Cadet Force) is a youth organisation that is sponsored by the MOD (Ministry Of Defence).
- The British Army is governed by the MOD and provides uniform and equipment for cadets and adult instructors.
- Military training areas and accommodation is also provided for a lot of cadet training.
- The ACF represents the British Army at lots of public events such as Remembrance day parades.
- Training is provided at local detachment training nights, during training weekends away and over a two week annual camp.

The APC syllabus - Star levels

- APC stands for Army Proficiency Certificate.
- When first starting as a cadet, you are a recruit cadet working towards becoming a basic cadet.
- After passing your basic training, you will be allowed to wear the 'basic' badge on your uniform and then work towards the next level which is one star.
- There are seven levels in total which are as follows:

NO BADGE **Recruit**

Basic

One star

Two star

Three star

Four star

Master cadet

The APC Syllabus

The APC syllabus is made up of ten core subjects which cover a selection of military subjects and increase in complexity the further you progress:

1. **Drill and Turnout**
   How cadets present themselves and move around when in a group.
2. **Military Knowledge**
   The history of the ACF and information about the modern army.
3. **Fieldcraft and tactics**
   Living out in the field and taking part in tactical, military style exercises.
4. **Navigation**
   Understanding and using different types of maps.
5. **Skill at arms**
   Learning about the weapons used in the ACF.
6. **Shooting**
   Firing the weapons used in the ACF at targets and in competition.
7. **First aid**
   Essential life saving skills.
8. **Physical training**
   Strength and cardio training needed for physical ACF activities.
9. **Expedition**
   Using various APC skills to walk and navigate long distances.
10. **Cadet in the community**
    Physically helping out with local events and projects.

Other APC subjects at certain detachments include music and signals.

Your detachment

As a new cadet, there is a lot to learn, but there are people here to help.

Fill in the names below:

Detachment commander (DC):

Second in command (2ic):

Sergeant instructor (SI):

Other instructors (include title):

Senior cadets (include title):

Here is a bit more for you to investigate.

Fill in the information below:

Fire alarm meeting point:

Detachment email address:

Detachment facebook page:

Parade nights and times:

First aiders name:

What does NAAFI stand for?:

CHAPTER TWO

Aim

By the end of this chapter, you will have received the following lessons:

1. The history of the ACF
2. Ranks and badges of rank

Instructors reference:

- Cadet training manual V1 - Chapter 3 - Sections 1 and 5

History of the ACF

- The ACF can trace its beginnings back to 1859 when there was a threat of invasion by the French.
- The ACF was properly formed in 1860.
- Octavia Hill was a pioneer of the ACF and introduced the standards seen today.
- At the start of the Boer war in 1899 there were around 50 schools with cadets.
- Initial cadet corps were in schools similar to modern day CCF units (Combined Cadet Force). The CCF also combine other military elements as well as the Army.
- In 1908 the term 'Cadet Force' was first used.
- During the first world war there was a big expansion of the cadet force.
- In 1930 the army stopped funding the cadet force and the British National Cadet Association (BNCA) took over and sought funding.
- In 1942, during the second world war, the ministry of defence resumed funding and providing uniforms.
- The second world war also saw another big expansion of the cadet force.
- In 1945, the BNCA became the Army Cadet Force Association (ACFA).
- In 1959 the cadet training centre at Frimley Park was opened.
- 1960 was the centenary of the ACF and HRH the Duke of Edinburgh presented the force with a special banner.
- There are now around 40,000 cadets in about 1,700 detachments in the UK.

Octavia Hill

Founded the Army cadet force in 1860

Ranks and badges of rank - Cadets

- The British army uses a rank structure to identify individuals that display leadership skills.
- A promotion is when someone is granted a higher rank.
- Higher ranks have more responsibility and are generally in charge of lower ranks.
- The army cadet force has its own rank structure for cadets, where promotion is based on the individual's leadership potential and responsible attitude.
- The rank structure is not based on APC progress, but a cadet must be at the required star level to achieve certain ranks.

Cadet rank structure:

Cadet
Lowest (starting) rank

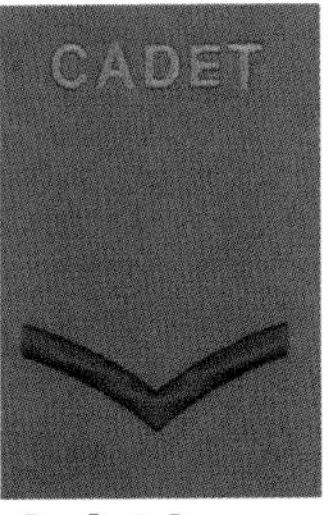

Cadet Lance Corporal
One star or above

Cadet Corporal
Two star or above

Cadet Sergeant
Three star or above

Cadet Staff (or Colour) Sergeant

Cadet Drum Major
Music units only

Cadet Sergeant Major

Cadet Regimental Sergeant Major
Highest cadet rank

Ranks and badges of rank - Instructors and army

Adult instructors have a rank structure that goes higher than cadets and is more in line with the regular army.

Probationary Instructor
(ACF only) Adult instructors in training.
1st and 2nd phase

Lance Corporal
Army only

Corporal
Army only

Sergeant
Instructor first rank

Staff (or Colour) Sergeant

Sergeant Major
Warrant officer class 2 (WO2)

Quarter Master Sergeant Major
Warrant officer class 2 (WO2)

Regimental Sergeant Major
Warrant officer class 1 (WO1)

- All ranks up to this level are called 'Non Commissioned Officers' (NCOs).

Under Officer
Probationary officer

Second Lieutenant

Lieutenant

Captain

Major

Lieutenant Colonel

Colonel

- All ranks after Under Officer are 'commissioned officers', meaning they have been commissioned by the Sovereign to do their job.

CHAPTER THREE: Drill and turnout

CHAPTER THREE

Aim

By the end of this chapter, you will have received the following lessons:

1. Turnout - Care and cleaning of uniform
2. The aim and purpose of drill
3. Positions of attention, stand at ease and stand easy
4. Turnings at the halt
5. Compliments - reasons, origins and information
6. Saluting to the front
7. Introduction to marching
8. Marching and halting in quick time

Instructors reference:

- Cadet training manual V1 - Chapter 1 & 2
- The Drill manual 1990

Turnout - Care and cleaning of uniform

- All cadets are issued with full uniform which includes everything except boots.
- The uniform is the same as the British army wears and is known as MTP-PCS.
- MTP = Multi Terrain Pattern - This is the camouflage pattern on clothing.
- PCS = Personal Clothing System - This is the name of the clothing system.

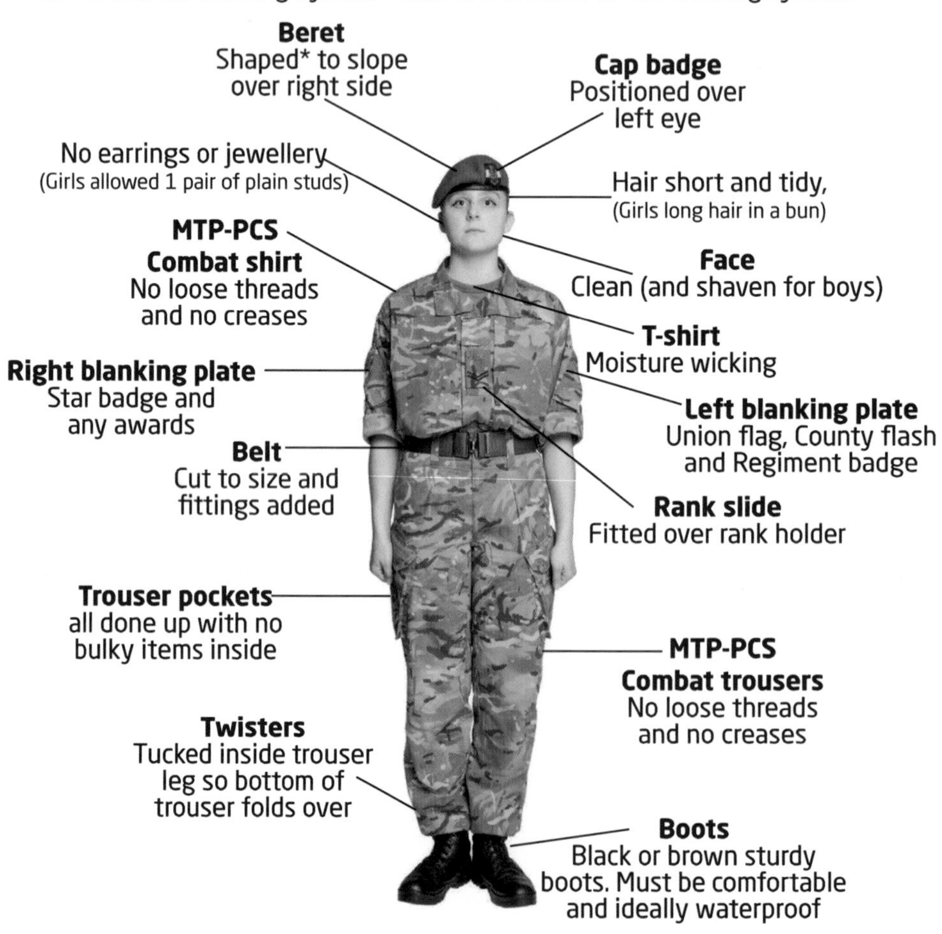

+ **MTP-PCS Combat jacket** - Worn for fieldcraft, shooting and as a warm top layer.

*Shaping a beret involves dunking the new beret into warm and then cold water repeatedly until thoroughly soaked (avoid getting the leather band wet). It is then placed on the head and pulled over to the right side to create the correct shape.

This should then be left to dry naturally before wearing.

Wearing, and caring for your uniform

- Cadets are privileged to be allowed to wear the uniform.
- Cadets represent the British Army so the utmost respect must be shown.
- Turnout and presentation should be impeccable at all times.
- Regular inspections are carried out on parade nights.
- Uniform must be kept clean and serviceable at all times.

Wash these in a washing machine on a medium setting:

- Combat shirt (empty pockets and remove blanking plates first)
- Combat trousers (empty pockets first)
- Combat jacket (empty pockets and remove blanking plates first)
- T-shirts

(Trousers, shirts and jackets should be ironed to remove all creases)

Boots and beret:

- Polish boots using a good brand polish of the correct colour.
- Brush off your beret, but don't wash it with your other clothing.

What are the current dress regulations?

Dress regulations change at certain times of the year, and for different areas of the country. Things that change include: Shirts tucked in or un-tucked. Sleeves rolled up or down.

Write your uniform sizes here along with current dress regulations:

Height:

Waist:

Seat:

Inside leg:

Head:

Chest:

Shoe size:

Current dress regulations:

The Aim & Purpose of Drill

Foot drill is made up of a series of standard moves that all cadets need to learn for use on parade at detachment, events or when away training.

Aim of drill

- To produce a cadet who is alert and obedient.
- Provides the basis of teamwork.

Purpose of drill

- Enable bodies of cadets to be moved easily and quickly from point to point in an orderly manner.
- Improves posture.
- Develops lungs and muscles.

Basic Drill movements

- Attention
- Stand at ease and stand easy
- Turnings at the halt
- Saluting
- Marching

Responding to words of command

When on parade 'words of command' are given in a specific way to ensure everyone reacts with the same movement at exactly the same time. Commands are given in a loud, clear manner and can be broken down into parts.

1. **Introductory:**
   - Normal paced command
   - Gives an indication of what drill move you are about to perform
   - E.G. **"TURNINGS AT THE HALT"**

2. **Cautionary:**
   - Drawn out (stretched) command
   - Prepares you to move
   - E.G. **" R I G H T "**

3. **Executive:**
   - Short sharp command
   - Gets immediate reaction from the entire squad
   - E.G. **"TURN"**

Attention

Eyes
Open and still looking just above your own height

Head
Held up with the neck touching the back of the collar

Chin
Tucked in with mouth closed

Shoulders
Held down and back to bring the chest to a normal position without straining

Arms
Straight and held to the sides with the forearm tucked in behind the hip bone

Wrists
Straight

Hands
Closed with the thumbs vertical and facing to the front. Backs of the fingers touching the thigh just behind the seam of the trousers

Knees
Braced with the body, upright and weight balanced evenly between the ball of the foot and the heel

Heels
Together with the feet turned out an angle of 30 degrees

Words of command:

"SQUAD"

" S Q U A D "

"SHUN"

Stand at ease

Head and upper body
Same as when at Attention

Feet
300mm apart (12 inches)

Arms
Behind the back and straight

Hands
Back of the right hand in the palm of the left hand

Thumbs
Cross the right thumb over the left thumb

Fingers
Straight and together

Stand easy

- On the command "stand easy" simply relax slightly in the 'at ease' position.
- On the command "Squad" brace back up into the 'at ease' position.

Moving between attention and stand at ease

- Keep the right foot still and leg braced back.
- Lift the left knee, then drive the left foot to the ground in the correct position (together for 'Attention' or apart for 'At Ease').
- At the same time force the arms into the correct position (to the side for 'Attention' or behind your back for 'At Ease').

Words of command:

"Stand"

" A T "

"EASE"

Turnings at the halt - Right (Left) turn

To learn how to turn correctly, we can break the movement into two parts:

Start in the 'Attention' position

Introductory: **"TURNING BY NUMBERS"**

Cautionary: **" R I G H T   T U R N "**

Executive: **"ONE"**

- Turn through 90 degrees to the right, using the right heel and left toes
- Keep the weight of the body on the right foot
- Keep both knees braced back, and body upright
- At the end of the movement the right foot is flat on the ground and the left leg is to the rear with the heel raised

Cautionary: **" S Q U A D "**

Executive: **"TWO"**

- Lift the left knee, then drive the left foot to the ground to resume the position of attention

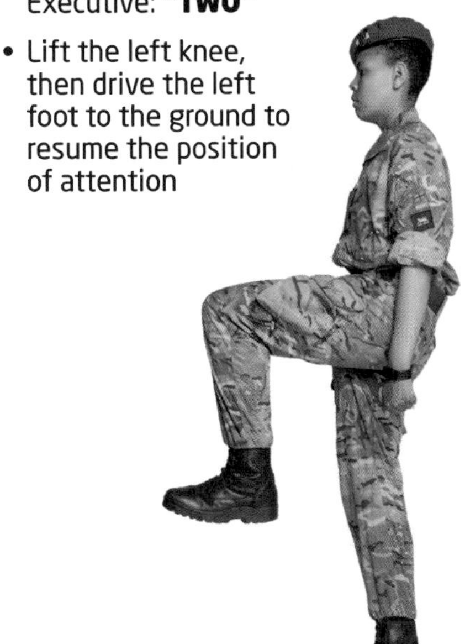

NOTE 1: When repeating the sequence use the commands: "Squad - One" "Squad - Two"

NOTE 2: When turning to the left, follow instructions above, but reverse all actions

Words of command for complete movement:

"TURNINGS AT THE HALT"

" R I G H T " **(or LEFT)**

"TURN"

Turnings at the halt - About turn

To learn how to about turn correctly, we can break the movement into two parts:

Start in the 'Attention' position

Introductory: **"TURNING BY NUMBERS"**

Cautionary: **"A B O U T T U R N"**

Executive: **"ONE"**

- Turn through 180 degrees to the right, using the right heel and left toe
- keep the weight of the body on the right foot
- Keep both knees braced back, and body upright
- At the end of the movement the right foot is flat on the ground and the left leg is to the rear with the heel raised

Cautionary: **"S Q U A D"**

Executive: **"TWO"**

- Lift the left knee, then drive the left foot to the ground to resume the position of attention

NOTE: When repeating the sequence use the commands: "Squad - One" "Squad - Two"

Words of command for complete movement

"Turnings at the halt"

"A B O U T"

"TURN"

Compliments - Reasons, origin and information

A compliment is a gesture made to show respect, that also shows loyalty and trust. There are three main types of compliments paid in the military:

1. **Salute with the hand**
2. **Salute with the sword**
3. **Present arms with a rifle**

Who and what do we pay compliments to?

Cadets learn the salute with the hand, and must pay this compliment to all officers they meet. In return, officers must return the compliment and salute back. (If not wearing head dress, do not salute, simply brace up into the attention position).

All compliments derive their origin from the Sovereign, to whom the highest compliment, the Royal Salute, is paid. Because of their link with the Sovereign the following are also paid some form of compliment:

1. **Members of the Royal Family**
2. **Governors and ministers to whom the Sovereign delegates authority**
3. **Formed bodies of troops on the Sovereign's business**
4. **All standards, guidons and colours of the Army and their equivalent in the Royal Navy, Royal Marines and Royal Air Force**
5. **All Officers, as holders of the Sovereign's commission**

When do we pay compliments?

1. **National Anthem**
   - On parade with an organised party, officers and warrant officers salute.
   - NCO's will only salute if they are in charge of the group.
   - When in uniform, but not on parade, all ranks will salute.
   - When not on parade or in uniform, simply stand to attention.
2. **Military Funerals** - Salute the bier (coffin)
3. **Passing standards, guidons and colours**
   - Entitled to the highest compliments.
   - Formed bodies on the march give eyes left/right.
   - Individuals will halt, and salute in the correct direction, or salute as passing.
4. **When boarding her Majesty's ships - Salute the quarterdeck**

Saluting to the front

To learn how to salute correctly, we can break the movement into two parts:

- Start in the 'Attention' position
- Introductory: **"SALUTING BY NUMBERS"**
- Cautionary: **"SALUTE TO THE FRONT"**
- Executive: **"ONE"**
- Raise the right arm sideways until it is horizontal

- Straighten the fingers and thumb keeping them together, with the palm facing the front
- Bend the elbow, keeping the hand and wrist straight until the tip of the forefinger is 25 mm (1 inch) above the right eye

Cautionary: **"SQUAD"**

Executive: **"TWO"**

- Return to the position of attention by dropping the elbow forward to the side of the body, then straighten the arm and close the hand

NOTE: When repeating the sequence use the commands: "Squad - One" "Squad - Two"

Words of command for complete movement

"SALUTING"

"SALUTE TO THE FRONT"

"SALUTE"

Introduction to marching

- Marching is a smart and uniformed way of walking.
- When moving around as a group, cadets will nearly always be required to march.
- Start by simply walking in time with other cadets, with an instructor or a senior cadet calling your left and right foot fall. As you gain confidence, start to move your arms more until your hands swing as high as your shoulder to the front and level with your waist to the rear. They should reach these points as your heel hits the ground.
- When marching in a group, you will be given the words of command "quick march". Immediately after this command you set off with your left foot while swinging your right arm to the front and pushing your left arm to the rear.

Words of command to commence marching

"BY THE LEFT" (or right)

" Q U I C K "

"MARCH"

Marching and halting in quick time

When commanded to halt while marching, it is important that everyone stops at exactly the same time with the same movements. The command can be given at any time, but is always given in time with the left foot hitting the ground.

The easiest way to explain how the process of halting works, is to talk through the words of command in time with which foot is on the ground when marching.

MARCHING (LEFT - RIGHT - LEFT - RIGHT)

LEFT - **" S Q U A D "**

RIGHT - (2)

LEFT - (3)

RIGHT - (4)

LEFT - **"HALT"**

RIGHT - (step) take one full pace

LEFT - (half) take one half pace

RIGHT - (stop) Bring right foot up to the left, stepping down firmly into the position of attention

Halting by numbers

To practice halting, the sequence can be broken down & practiced by three counts:

1. On the word of command **"HALT"**, everyone freezes with their left foot forward
2. **"SQUAD HALT ONE"** Take one full pace forward with the right foot
3. **"SQUAD TWO"** Take a half pace forward with the left foot
4. **"SQUAD THREE"** Bring right foot up to the left, stepping down firmly into The position of attention

Aim

By the end of this chapter, you will have received the following lessons:

1. Fieldcraft - Overview
2. Preparation and packing of equipment

CHAPTER FOUR

Instructors reference:

- Fieldcraft manual
- Fieldcraft Tactics (syllabus)

Fieldcraft - Overview

Fieldcraft covers everything to do with military life outdoors. Being 'out in the field' means that you are away from modern facilities and have to operate and survive with just whatever you can carry and take with you. This can be in woodland, fields or even mountainous areas.

This is a general overview of what fieldcraft is about:

- Looking after yourself and your equipment
- Providing your own food and shelter
- How to move and observe without being seen
- Observing, and judging distances
- Moving around in a section and patrolling
- Operating outside at night
- Reacting to enemy fire and contact with an enemy
- Defending against attack and using sentries

There are many lessons covering different aspects of fieldcraft, but most are hands on and are lots of fun. As you progress through the APC syllabus, fieldcraft training is more about practical application of skills learnt as well as the development of leadership skills.

Here is a breakdown of what to expect at each star level:

Basic training: Preparation and packing of personal equipment, ready for fieldcraft training.

One star training: How to be self-reliant in the field and look after yourself and your own equipment. You will also learn the basic skills needed to operate as a rifleman within a section.

Two star training: Further training will give you better understanding of patrolling and patrol harbours. Your skills as a rifleman will be developed to allow you to take part in recce patrols, standing patrols and the occupation of patrol harbours.

Three star training: Your skills as a rifleman will be further developed to allow you to take part in fighting patrols and contact with the enemy and attacks in various situations. You will also be introduced to basic leadership skills.

Four star training: At this point all major topics will have been covered, so the emphasis will now be on leadership and the ability to lead a section of cadets.

Preparation and packing of equipment - CEFO

When training out in the field, there are certain items you will need to take with you. The items you need depend on the type of training you are doing and how long you will be away from camp for.

C - Complete

E - Equipment

F - Fighting

O - Order

- This is the minimum you will take in the field or onto a shooting range.
- You will only take essential items so that you can move and work a lot easier.
- Not suitable for extended or overnight exercises.
- Everything should be packed so as not to rattle and make noise when moving.
- Items that may get damaged by water should be placed into waterproof bags.

PLCE Webbing (PLCE = Personal Load Carrying Equipment)

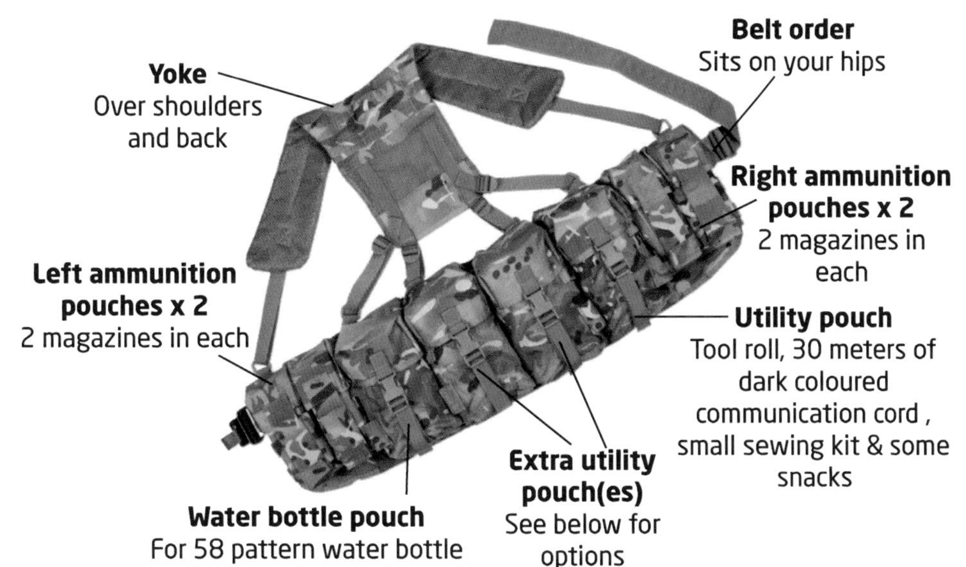

Possible extra items for utility pouches:

- Cold weather gear (hat, gloves, scarf etc.)
- Warm weather gear (sun cream, bush hat etc.)
- Foot gear (spare socks, laces, foot powder etc.)
- KFS (Knife, Fork & Spoon)
- Torch and spare batteries
- Personal first aid kit

CEMO

When taking part in longer exercises where you will be required to stay out over night, more equipment is needed, so you need more carrying capacity.

C - Complete

E - Equipment

M - Marching

O - Order

- This is everything you need to survive and operate for longer than one day.
- You will only take essential items so that you are not carrying too much.
- Items that may get damaged by water should be placed into waterproof bags.

Bergen

Extra items to pack:

- Small wash kit (toothbrush/paste soap etc.)
- Boot cleaning kit (polish, brush and cloth)
- Rubbish bag
- KFS (Knife, Fork & Spoon)
- Mess tins, rations and cooker
- Personal first aid kit

Extras & alternatives

When training out in the field or on a range there are a few extra essentials you will need as well as some alternatives that can be considered.

MTP-PCS Combat Jacket

Needs to be with you when in the field or on a range

- Note book and pen/pencil
- Compass
- Spare spoon
- Tissues/toilet paper
- Whistle
- Torch (with red light)
- Gloves
- Cam cream

Daysack

Useful for full days of training when not staying out overnight

- Waterproof clothing
- Warm top or fleece
- Cold/warm weather gear
- Personal first aid kit
- Torch & spare batteries
- Snacks and extra water

Assault vest

An alternative to webbing - pack the same as CEFO

Staying away from home

Most fieldcraft exercises and a lot of range days will occur as part of an extended time away from home, either over a weekend or a two week camp.

When not sleeping out in the field, you will most likely be based at a regular army camp, sleeping in normal beds, so will need extra items to those already listed.

Clothing - Dependant on length of stay

- Uniform (trousers, shirt, t-shirt, beret, twisters, rank slide, belt, jacket, boots)
- Spare uniform (trousers, shirts, t-shirts)
- Spare boots if you have them (especially if out in the field and in the classroom)
- Civilian (civvy) clothes and shoes for evening wear and/or adventurous activities
- Spare underwear
- Spare socks
- Extra cold weather clothing if it's cold (fleece, hat, gloves etc.)
- Sun screen and jungle hat if it's warm
- Physical Training (PT) clothing and trainers

Sleeping

- Sleeping bag or duvet (for in camp)
- Pillow case
- Duvet cover

Extras

- Wash kit (shower gel, shaving kit, deodorant, toothpaste, toothbrush, wet wipes)
- Towel and flannel
- Money (just enough for your time away)
- Mobile phone & charger
- Note books and pens
- Padlock for locker
- Any personal medicine/tablets (to be handed in to staff to look after)

Speak to the staff and senior cadets at your detachment to find out any other items you may need while away and write them down in this box:

Aim

By the end of this chapter, you will have received the following lessons:

1. Introduction to maps; Care and use of maps
2. Introduction to handrails and map orientation
3. Using handrails and maintaining position with an orientated map

Instructors reference:

- ACF Training manual
- ISPEC numbers 1 - 3
- Navigation handbook

Introduction to maps; Care and use of maps

What is a map?

- A map is a birds-eye view of a piece of land scaled down to a manageable size.
- Maps are only 100% accurate at the time of manufacture.
- Can be extremely accurate or just give a general guide.
- Information shown and scale varies dependant on the type of map.

Types of maps include:

- Street maps
- Road maps
- Town/shopping centre maps
- Local attraction maps
- Ordnance Survey maps
- Military maps
- Sketch maps
- Atlas/world maps
- Google maps

Looking after maps

- Maps can be expensive to buy and if damaged are expensive to replace.
- You can be in actual danger if you get lost and are unable to read your map.
- Maps can be waterproofed by laminating, placing into a waterproof bag or keeping in a map case.

DO	**DO NOT**
Fold maps correctly	Screw maps up
Waterproof maps	get maps wet
Write on plastic map covers only	Write on maps directly

How to fold a map

When a map is folded correctly, it is possible to view a small area of the map without having to open it out completely.

1. Start with you map facing up and fold it in half length ways.

* Fold the map so that you can still see the map detail

FULL MAP

FOLD IN HALF

2. Fold the map in half again, but from left to right this time

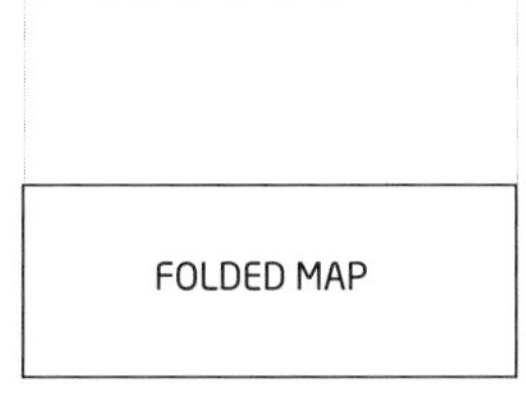

FOLD IN HALF AGAIN

3. Open the map back out to the previous stage and then fold the left and right sides back on them selves into the middle

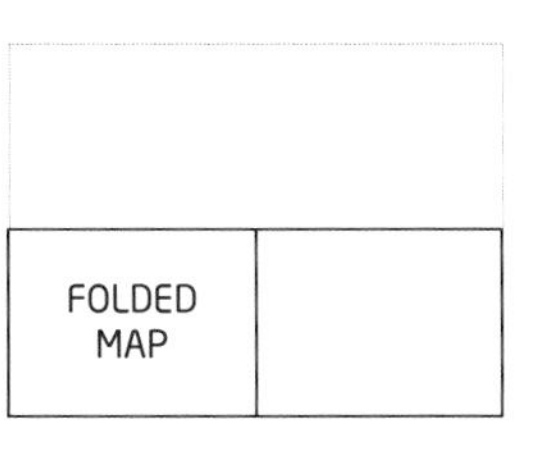

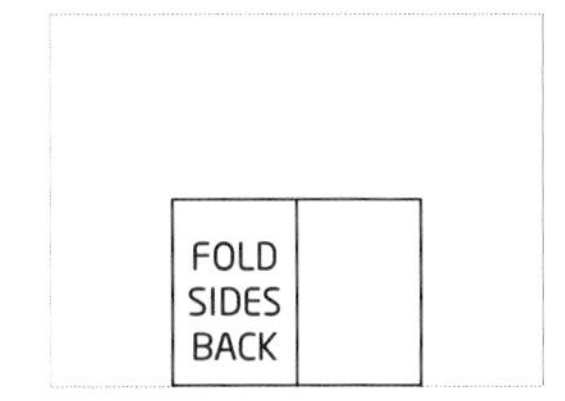

4. Your map is now folded in a concertina, which allows you to view any part of the map without opening it fully

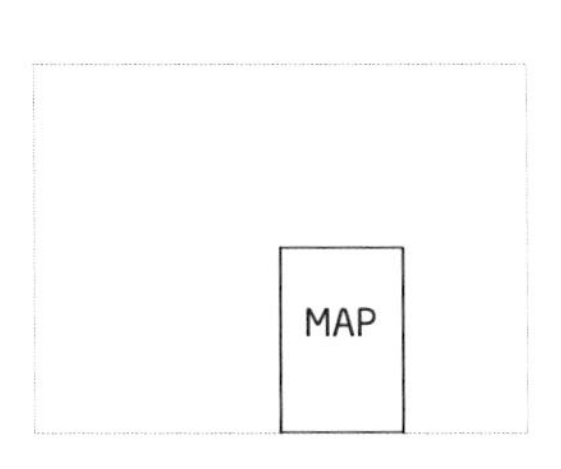

FRONT | INSIDE LEFT | INSIDE RIGHT | BACK

Larger maps may need more folds, so continue in the same way until correct.

Map information and marginal information

Maps contain lots of information that can help us navigate and explore.
Most general maps have some or all of the following information:

- Roads
- Footpaths
- Rivers
- Train lines
- Hills
- Lakes
- Towns

Look at a selection of maps and see how many other things you can see on them.

Marginal information

Maps nearly always have some information about the map to make it easier to read. This is normally in one place, to the side or above/below the main map and is called 'marginal information'.

Marginal information has some or all of the following:

- Map scale
- Date of creation
- Area covered
- Key to map symbols
- Magnetic north

Look again at your selection of maps and see how much more information there is.

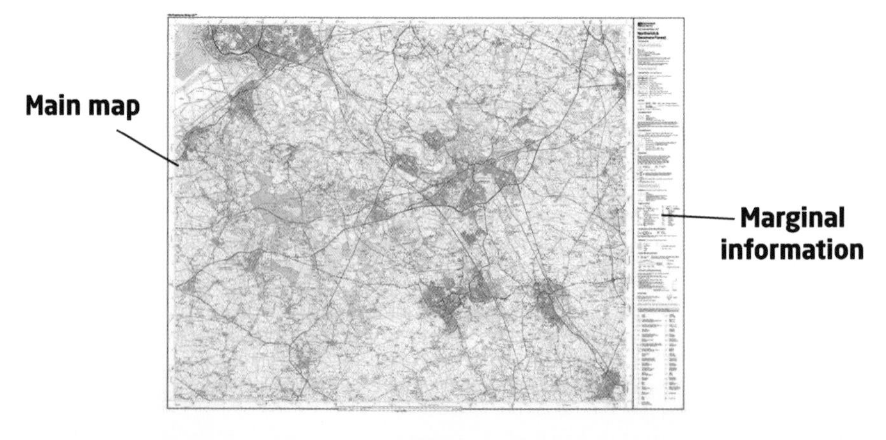

Introduction to handrails and map orientation

Handrails

A handrail is a linear feature that appears on the ground and on a map. It can be followed to assist navigation. Examples of handrails are:

- Roads
- Paths
- Tracks
- Hedges
- Tree lines
- Railway lines
- Hills and slopes

Look at your selection of maps again to see how many handrails you can identify.

Map orientation

- A map should be read so that the features line up with what is on the ground.
- The writing on a map may end up being upside down or sideways.
- When a map is orientated with the ground, you will move around the map and the map will stay in the same position.

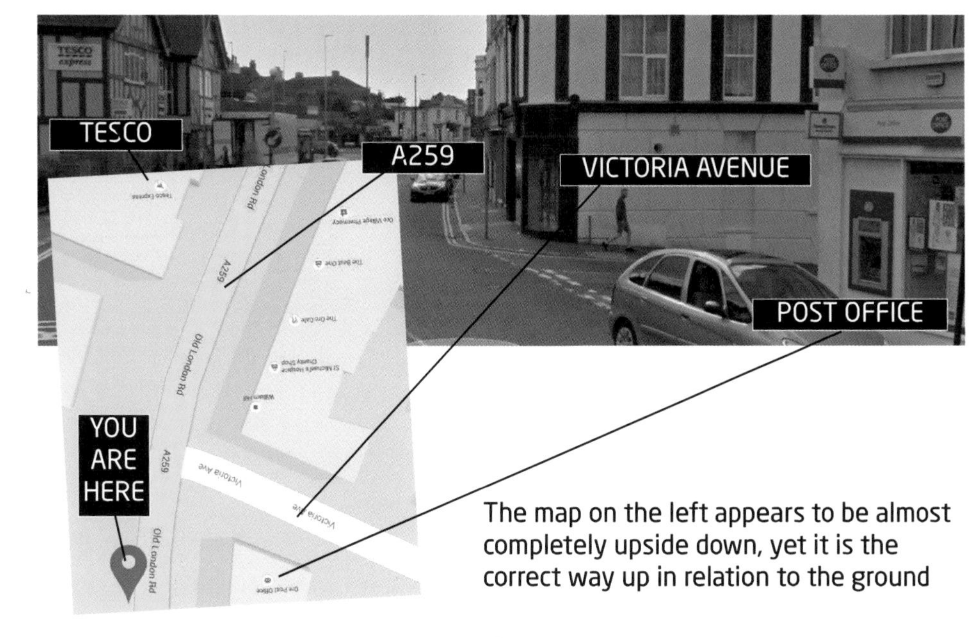

The map on the left appears to be almost completely upside down, yet it is the correct way up in relation to the ground

Using handrails and maintaining position

Following handrails are a great way of navigating, but on some longer handrails such as paths and tracks, it is important to know how far along you are to be able to make turns or find your destination.

Collecting Features

To do this we use 'collecting features' which are things we pass and can check off or 'collect' as we follow a handrail along a route.

Example:
Look at the street map to the right.

- You are in town and you need to get to the theatre.
- Your are outside the bakers, so looking on your map you can see that the bakers needs to be on your left hand side and the butchers on your right for you to head in the correct direction.
- To confirm your location, you look at your surroundings and then orientate your map, so that what you see around you matches the map.
- On the map, you can see that you need to walk along the road, passing the cafe and then the library on your left.
- The theatre will then be on your left opposite the doctors.

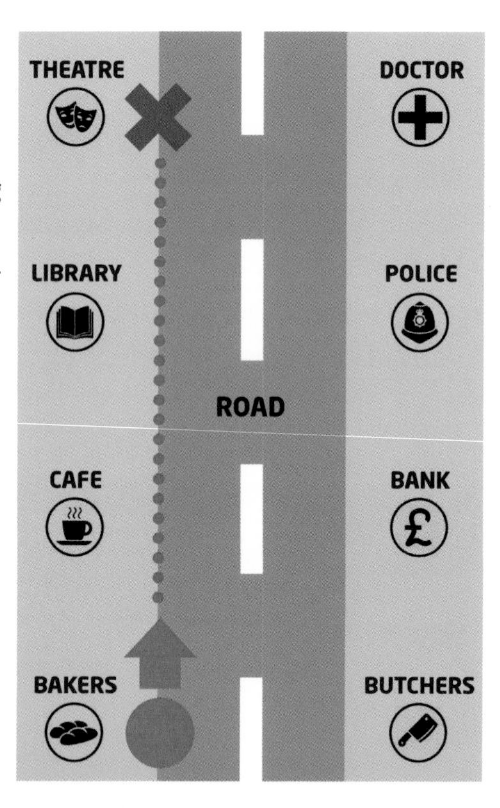

To help you find your way you have used the road as a handrail and the bakers, cafe, library and doctors as collecting features. You could have also used the bank and police station to double check your location.

Maintaining position

As you walk the route, you would also place your thumb over each location as you pass it so that you know where you are. This is known as 'maintaining position'.

Map symbols as handrails and collecting features

You will notice on the street map on the previous page there are small pictures which represent each building that is labelled. These are called map symbols and even if each place wasn't labelled, you would probably know what it was just from the picture.

Map symbols are used on nearly all maps, as they are easy to identify and don't require lots of words to label things. Here are a small selection of map symbols from an Ordnance Survey (OS) map:

Handrails:

Trunk or main road

Footpath

Electricity Transmission line

Collecting features:

Telephone

Picnic site

Place of worship

Some are both:

Some features can be used as either a handrail or a collecting feature.

For example, the symbol to the right is for a wooded area or forest. You could use the edge of a forest as a handrail to follow, or passing an area of woodland can be used as a collecting feature.

Coniferous trees

Applying lessons to a real map

Now that you understand about handrails, collecting features, orientating a map and maintaining position, take a look at the small section of map below and identify as many handrails and collecting features as you can. Work in pairs or small groups and take it in turns at giving directions between two various points using all that you have learnt so far.

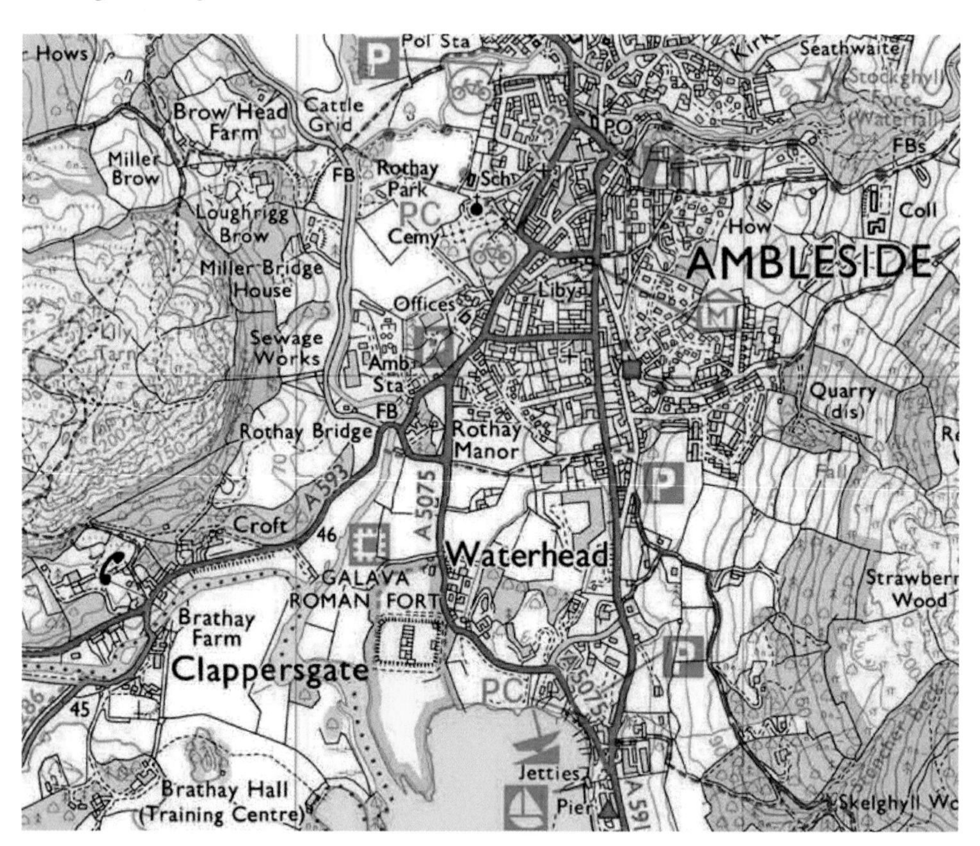

When you are happy with the theory, you need to put it into practice outside with a real map. Work with an instructor and other cadets and navigate short distances remembering the following key points:

- Orientate your map to the ground
- Follow handrails
- Use collecting features along your route
- Keep your thumb on your last known location to maintain position

CHAPTER SIX: Expedition

CHAPTER SIX

Aim

By the end of this chapter, you will have received the following lessons:

1. Expedition - Overview
2. Using the countryside

Instructors reference:

- ACF Manual
- Expedition training syllabus
- DofE Website

Expedition - Overview

Expedition Training involves working as a team to navigate routes of at least 8km, setting up campsites and will usually include staying out at least one night. It also combines skills learnt through first aid, navigation and fieldcraft.

It is essential for cadets to receive sufficient training in the subjects below so the risks of any potentially dangerous situations are reduced.

Basic Training

- **Using the Countryside:**
  Understand how to treat land and property with respect.

One star training

- **Building the Team:**
  Work as a member of a team and support other team members.

- **Expedition Equipment:**
  Using the correct clothing and equipment to ensure the expedition is carried out in comfort and safety.

- **Load Carrying:**
  Carry the required load without causing exhaustion or injury.

- **The Camp Site:**
  Understanding how to live outdoors in safety and comfort.

- **Food and Cooking:**
  How to prepare and eat a nourishing meal.

- **Debriefing:**
  To reflect on the expedition and learn lessons from the experience.

Duke of Edinburgh Award (DofE)

DofE is one of the world's most popular development programmes for young people aged 14-24.

The DofE Award includes four categories of highly practical, cultural and adventurous activities. Most of these are cross-related with the ACF activities covered in the APC Syllabus. So whilst training for first aid, drill, target shooting and expeditions, cadets can also working towards a DofE Award.

The Awards are well regarded and recognised by universities and employers.

Levels

There are three levels of Award: Bronze, Silver and Gold. For each level, four sections need to be completed:

- **Volunteering**
- **Physical**
- **Skills**
- **Expedition**

(The Gold Award also includes completing a Residential section).

Using the countryside

The Countryside Code - Respect. Protect. Enjoy.

- **Respect other people:**
- **Protect the natural environment:**
- **Enjoy the outdoors:**

It is important to obey the Countryside Code at all times including when out training. The following topics relate to the expected behaviour of cadets when in the countryside, these are based on advice given in the Countryside Code.

Respect other countryside users:

- Noise. Shouting, loud singing, audible music, etc. are an intrusion on the wish of many to enjoy the peace and quiet of the countryside.
- Litter. Discarded wrappers, fruit peel and other waste spoils the beauty of the countryside and may be harmful to animals. Keep your litter with you until you can dispose of it in the appropriate container.

Respect those who work in the countryside

- Co-operate with farm workers gathering or moving animals.
- Do not walk over growing crops. This includes grass grown as fodder.
- Leave gates as you find them, unless it is obvious it has been left open accidentally.
- Keep out of farm buildings, and away from farm machinery.

Protect the natural environment:

- Take all steps to prevent fire. Remember broken glass can start fires from the rays of the sun.
- Take care not to damage buildings, historic sites, etc.
- Use footpaths and bridleways except where open access is permitted. Be aware that landowners may deny access at certain times of the year.
- Protect water supplies.

Aim

By the end of this chapter, you will have received the following lessons:

1. Introduction to shooting in the ACF
2. Safety with weapons
3. Rules for firing on .22 and air rifle ranges
4. The air rifle - Overview
5. The L144A1 CSBTR - General description, safety and sights
6. Stripping, assembly, cleaning and maintenance
7. Basic handling drills, firing and stoppages
8. Zeroing
9. Marksmanship principles - Overview

Instructors reference:

- ACF SAA Shooting manual
- APC (ACF) syllabus shooting
- Air rifle publication-05-aug2014
- AC72027_L144A1 CSBTR Manual

ALL SKILL AT ARMS LESSONS MUST BE TAUGHT BY A QUALIFIED SKILL AT ARMS INSTRUCTOR - THIS CHAPTER PROVIDES REVISION ONLY

Introduction to shooting in the ACF

Weapon training is broken down into two subjects. Skill at arms and shooting.

Skill at arms

Lessons look at the safety, handling and operation of the following weapons at their respective star levels:

- **Recruit cadets (Basic training)** - .22 rifle and/or air rifle
- **One star and two star training cadets** - Cadet GP rifle (L98 A2 Cadet GP)
- **Three star training cadets** - LSW (Light Support Weapon) and target rifle

Shooting

This is where you actually get to fire the weapons at targets on a range. Shooting is progressive, and distances fired over and expected standards of shooting is raised in accordance with your training level.

- **Recruit cadets (Basic training)**
  .22 rifle fired at a range of 25 meters with reasonable accuracy
  or
  .177 air rifle fired at a range of 8 meters with reasonable accuracy.
- **One star training cadets**.
  .22 rifle fired at a range of 25 meters with good accuracy.
- **Two star training cadets**
  Cadet GP rifle fired at a range of 100 meters with good accuracy.
- **Three star training cadets**
  Cadet GP rifle or LSW or cadet Target rifle fired at various distances and from different positions.
- **Four star training cadets** - To pass four star training cadets get to choose from various subjects to specialise in. If shooting is chosen, then competition standard accuracy is expected on all weapons.

Competition shooting

The cadet target rifle is open to cadets of any level that display good shooting skills and can pass the relevant handling tests. Competition shoots range from 100 - 1000 meters and can lead to competitions abroad.

Shooting in the ACF can also contribute to the **Duke of Edinburgh's award scheme** which is an award achieved by taking part in several activities. Shooting comes under 'volunteering', 'skills' and 'residential'.

Safety with weapons

Handling of weapons within the ACF is completely safe, as long as certain safety procedures are followed. All weapons used can be potentially lethal and although under constant supervision from adult instructors, cadets need to learn, understand and adhere to ALL safety precautions. Failure to do so may result in serious injury.

The six rules

1. **A weapon must never be pointed at anyone in any circumstances.**
2. **A weapon must always be handled so that it points in such a direction that there is no danger if a round is accidentally fired.**
3. **Whenever a weapon is picked up which has not been under an individual's direct supervision, it must be examined to make sure it is not loaded *NSPs (Normal Safety Precautions) must be carried out.**
4. **Whenever a weapon is handed to someone else, the recipient must first be shown that it is unloaded (clear). The recipient must insist that he/she is shown that the weapon is unloaded.**
5. **The muzzle of a weapon must never be rested against any part of the body.**
6. **A weapon must be in the unloaded state prior to traveling in a vehicle or during non tactical moves on foot.**

Safety with weapons - ammunition

- The CSBTR requires each round to be hand fed into the chamber.
- Ammunition is to be handled with extreme care and never be held in the hand for longer than it takes to prepare the required rounds for a shoot, or when loading.
- Ammunition should be kept clean and dry.
- Never attempt to fire any rounds that have been involved in a stoppage or misfire.

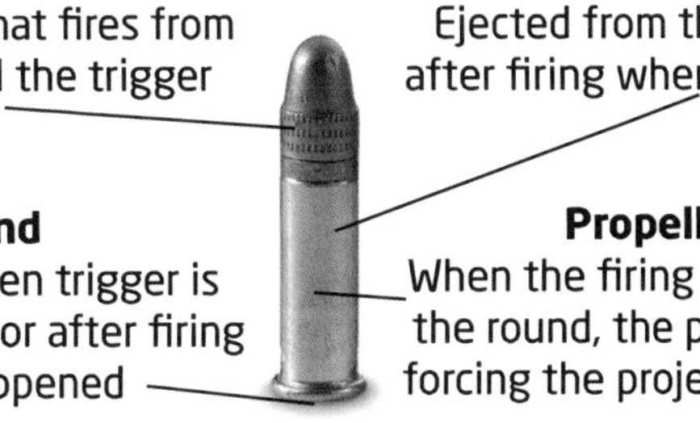

Projectile
The part of the round that fires from the rifle when you pull the trigger

Brass case
Ejected from the side of the rifle after firing when the bolt is opened

Base of round
Struck by firing pin when trigger is pulled. Grabbed by ejector after firing when the bolt is opened

Propellant inside
When the firing pin hits the base of the round, the propellant explodes, forcing the projectile out of the rifle

Rules for firing on .22 and air rifle Ranges

When you are familiar with a weapon and have passed the relevant weapon handling test, you will then be able to fire it on a miniature range. There are not many rules to remember and you will always be guided by the official range staff.

Official range staff:

- Range Conducting Officer (RCO) - Over all in charge of the range and safety
- Safety supervisors
- Coaches (adults or experienced cadets)

Miniature range rules:

- Only the CSBTR, the air rifle or the L98 A2 with a .22 conversion can be fired.
- Only official range staff and cadets firing are allowed on the firing point.
- Ammunition will be issued only on the firing point by an adult instructor.
- No weapon will be loaded without orders from the RCO.
- Firing indiscriminate dry shots is forbidden other than for the firing of dry shots. at the beginning of a practice, if authorised by the RCO.
- The muzzle of a rifle will at all times be pointed towards the bullet catcher. This includes loading, firing, unloading and inspecting.
- At the conclusion of any firing when it is necessary to examine the targets, rifles will be unloaded and laid on the firing point with breeches open. The firers will stand up behind the firing point. No individual will move forward until the RCO has ensured that all weapons have been inspected and are clear.
- As each detail finishes firing and after the weapons have been inspected (see above), live rounds and empty cases will be collected and separated under the orders of the RCO. When this has been completed, he may order the firers forward to examine their targets, or have them brought to the firing point.
- No one will be allowed to fire or to spectate on a .22 range unless they are wearing approved ear protection.

End of shoot declaration:

At the conclusion of all firing, the RCO will inspect all weapons and equipment to ensure that the weapons are unloaded and clear and that the firers are not in possession of any live ammunition or empty cases. The RCO will then read a warning to the cadets to which each cadet must make a declaration individually.

Each individual will declare:

- "I have no ammunition in my possession and I will report anyone else who has".

OR

- "I have no pellets in my possession".

The air rifle - Overview

The air rifle is potentially the first weapon you will get to fire as a cadet. It is simple to operate and will allow you to learn and practice the marksmanship principles.

There are two air rifles available, both of which are very similar to operate.

1. BSA Scorpion Cadet .177
2. Air Arms CZ 200 Cadet .177

They are both bolt operated, magazine fed weapons that use air to fire pellets at a range of 6.5 - 10 metres. The air is pumped into a cylinder fixed to the rifle (always done by an adult instructor). They both fire .177 calibre air rifle pellets.

BSA Scorpion Cadet .177 rifle

(Parts are the same for the Air Arms CZ 200 Cadet .177 rifle)

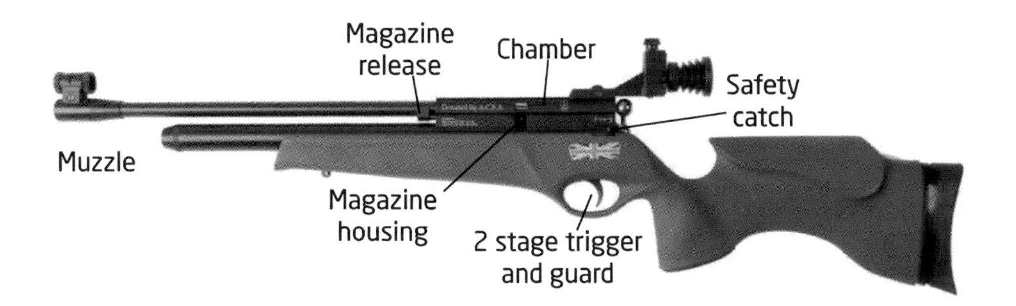

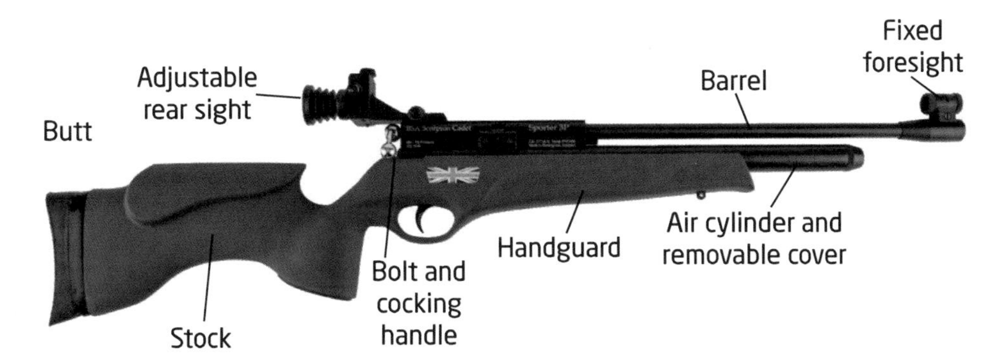

Before and after firing, ensure the cartridge platform, breech and ejector are clean and free from debris.

The L144 A1 Cadet Small Bore Target Rifle (CSBTR)

The L144 A1 Cadet Small Bore Target Rifle (CSBTR) will be one of the first weapons you get to fire, and is the perfect weapon to help learn the basics of shooting. Before firing it though, there are some key lessons that need to be learnt and a weapon handling test to pass.

The CSBTR is a bolt action, manually fed weapon system that needs to be loaded after each round has been fired. It is fitted with iron sights that are accurate up to 25 metres, and can be fired indoors or outdoors on approved purpose built ranges only.

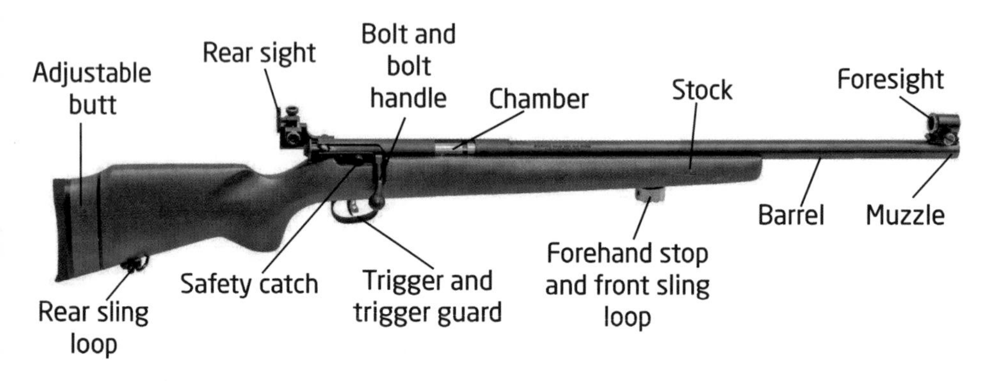

Features of CSBTR:

- Adjustable butt extension - Allows the length of the rifle to be adjusted quickly and easily to suit all sizes of cadets.
- Forehand stop - Set a specific position for the forehand to go and lock it in place. Numbers underneath help cadets remember their personal settings.
- Adjustable rear sights - Allow rifles to be zeroed to each individual cadet, allowing for greater accuracy when firing at competition targets. Eye relief can also be adjusted.
- Foresight elements - Can change between aperture and post elements.
- Easy to see safety catch. Red dot showing = Not safe. 'S' showing = Safe.
- Red coloured feed tray - The inside of the chamber is coloured red to highlight if the rifle is loaded or not when the bolt is open.
- Rifle stand to rest the weapon when not firing (not to be used when firing).
- Single piece web material sling - Can be used to provide greater support when firing.

Normal Safety Precautions - NSPs

NSPs are to be carried out on all weapons on the following occasions:

- At the beginning of any lesson, practice period or range period.
- When picking up a rifle that hasn't been under your direct supervision.
- When handing over a rifle, or receiving it from someone else.

Normal Safety Precautions for the CSBTR

On the command 'For inspection - port arms'

1. **Take control of the weapon, ensuring it is pointing in a safe direction.**
2. **Keep the weapon horizontal to the ground with your right hand holding the small of the butt, finger outside the trigger guard, and your Left hand supporting the stock.**
3. **With the right hand, raise the bolt and pull to the rear. Set safety catch to safe ('S' showing), then inspect the face of the bolt, body and chamber to ensure they are clear.**
4. **In low light a torch may be required, it may also be necessary to feel the breech, face of the bolt and chamber with a finger to ensure they are clear.**

The instructor will show his weapon is clear to a member of the squad, and then check all cadet's weapons to make certain they are also clear.

On the command 'Ease springs'

5. **Keep the weapon pointing in a safe direction.**
6. **With the right hand, thrust the bolt handle forward then down making sure the bolt is fully closed. Set safety catch to fire (red dot showing).**
7. **Ensure trigger finger is square over the 'accurelease' located within the trigger and operate the trigger to fire off the action (if finger is not in the correct position, the action may not fire off correctly, repeat whole process if this happens).**

When on a range, drills will be carried out in the prone position.

Safe handling

When handing a weapon over to someone else, carry out stages 1 - 4 and then show the recipient for them to inspect. When satisfied they will confirm "clear". Continue with stages 5 - 7 before handing the weapon over.

Stripping, assembly, cleaning and maintenance

To keep weapons in good condition and make sure they continue to work, it is important that they are well maintained and cleaned. A build up of debris can lead to malfunction and misfires and can ultimately be dangerous.

Rules for stripping and assembly

- Follow the correct sequence.
- Do not attempt to do more than you have been taught.
- Only strip and assemble when needed, to avoid wear.
- Report any defects or damage immediately.
- DO NOT swap parts between rifles.
- Before attempting to strip the weapon, carry out a full NSP and remove the sling.

Stripping and assembly

- Sights - Only CFAVs or senior cadets can remove, and only if essential.
- Bolt assembly - Can be removed, but not stripped further by cadets.
- Serial numbers - Make sure barrel and bolt have the same serial number.
- Function test - After assembly, carry out a full function test to check working.

Cleaning and maintenance

- Only used approved products for cleaning and oiling parts.
- Never use abrasive materials.
- Clean the bore with the cleaning rod and brush or jag from the chamber end.
- Flannelette used to clean the bore with the jag must be 50mm x 30mm.
- Flannelette with or without oil can be used to clean the bolt assembly, chamber, breach and other metal parts.
- Use a soft brush to remove any loose fouling or debris.
- Frequency and level of cleaning will depend on what use it has had. After firing on a range it will need more cleaning than after a skill at arms lesson or after a period in an armoury.
- For normal daily use, lubrication can be applied to the bolt assembly, chamber and breach area and bore. The rear sight adjustment screws can also be lubricated.
- Make sure there is no excess oil or water present when firing as this can be dangerous and can lead to damage of the rifle.
- When firing in poor weather conditions keep the bolt closed when possible to stop water entering the rifle. Clean and dry thoroughly after to avoid rust.

Basic handling drills, firing and stoppages

Preparing the weapon for firing

- Feed tray and bolt face - Ensure they are free from oil and are dry.
- Bolt assembly - Lightly lubricate the surfaces on the moving parts.
- Ammunition - Needs to be clean and dry.
- Eye relief - The rear sight can be adjusted to ensure the optimum distance of 25mm from the eye is achieved .
- Sights - Reset rear sight adjustments to their central position (see 'Zeroing').
- Extendable butt - Adjust to each cadets physical build (return to closed position before returning to the armoury).
- Forehand stop - Adjust to each cadets physical build to assist in holding the weapon. A glove may need to be worn when using this feature.
- Sling - When using for support, adjust the length to suit each individual cadet.

Load, ready and unload (words of command)

When firing any weapon on a live range, there are set words of command to let you know what to do and when to do it. For safety reasons it is extremely important that you understand these commands and act accordingly.

"Prone position - down"

1. Carefully get down into the prone (lying down) position and take control of the weapon. Keep finger off of the trigger and set up a comfortable firing position.

"Load"

1. Support the stock with the left hand.
2. With the right hand, raise the bolt and pull to the rear. Set safety catch to safe ('S' showing).
3. With the right hand, pick up one round and check it is clean and undamaged before placing it into the chamber on the feed tray.
4. Carefully move the bolt forward, this will cause the round to be fed into the chamber.
5. With the bolt fully forward, push the bolt handle down to lock it into position.
6. The weapon is now 'loaded' and made 'ready'.

"Test and adjust"

1. Build up the position and hold of the weapon, and aim correctly at the target.

"Fire"

1. Ensure sights are set correctly.
2. Move safety catch to fire (red dot exposed).
3. Ensure position and hold are correct.
4. Move the trigger finger onto the trigger and start the firing cycle.
5. After each shot, repeat steps 1 - 5 of the 'load' procedure. This will eject an empty case each time.

"Stop"

1. If you have not finished firing, set safety catch to safe ('S') and await instructions.

"Unload"

1. With the right hand, raise the bolt and pull to the rear. Set safety catch to safe ('S' showing). A round or empty case may be ejected at this time (hand in at end).
2. Tilt the weapon to the left and look inside, ensuring the feed tray, chamber and face of the bolt are clear.
3. Close the bolt, move the safety catch to fire (red dot exposed) and pull the trigger.

The rifle is now unloaded. Await further instructions.

Immediate action (IA) and stoppage drills

There may be instances when the rifle doesn't fire. This can be for various reasons, but in most cases this can be resolved by the person firing.

If the rifle fails to fire, the following drills should be carried out:

1. Tap the bolt down to ensure it has closed properly, then fire again.

If this resolves the problem and the weapon now fires, no further action is required. If the weapon still fails to fire, continue with these next steps:

2. With the right hand, raise the bolt and pull to the rear. Set safety catch to safe ('S' showing) and look into the chamber.

If the chamber is clear, load a new round, continue with the load procedure and continue to fire.

If the chamber is not clear and there is a round or case in the chamber that hasn't extracted, close and open the bolt again to attempt to clear the obstruction. If the round or case now ejects, put it to one side, load a new round, continue with the load procedure and continue to fire.

If an obstruction doesn't clear, or if the rifle still fails to fire, alert a member of the range staff. DO NOT attempt to fire any rounds involved in a stoppage.

Zeroing

Everyone that fires a weapon will have their own way of aiming through the sights to align with a target. This means that 2 firers of equal skill can fire the same weapon and aim at the same point on a target but their rounds may fall in different places. This does not mean either of the firers are bad, it just means that the sights have not been adjusted specifically for them. This is where 'zeroing' a weapon's sights to the firer comes in.

Grouping

If after firing several rounds at a target, you see that all of your shots are really close together, but are not exactly where you aimed, this means that you are potentially a good shot, but the rifle sights are not zeroed to you. In some firing practices, this doesn't matter as the closeness of the shots to each other is the most important factor.

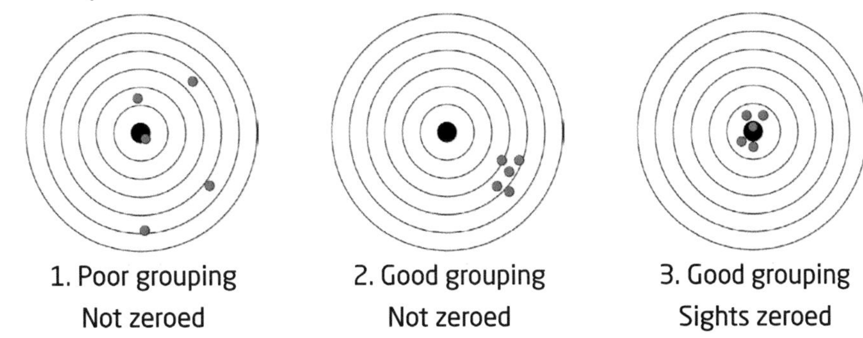

1. Poor grouping Not zeroed

2. Good grouping Not zeroed

3. Good grouping Sights zeroed

In all of the examples above, the firer was aiming at the bottom centre of the centre black dot.

Example 1 shows poor shooting skills, and the sights have not been zeroed to the firer. Example 2 shows good shooting skills, but the sights have still not been zeroed to the firer. Example 3 shows good shooting skills and the sights have been zeroed to the firer.

Zeroing the sight

Zeroing the sights to the firer, simply means adjusting them to compensate for any difference in the firers point of aim and where the rounds actually fall.

In example 2 above, the firer has achieved a good group size (shots are close together), but they all fall slightly down and right of the centre of the target (the point of aim). The sights therefore need to be adjusted left and up to allow the firer to aim at the same point, yet get the rounds closer to the centre of the target. Example 3 then shows what the same group fired from a correctly zeroed weapon with the same point of aim.

On the CSBTR this is achieved by adjusting the rear sight, and will be done for you by a CFAV or senior cadet.

Marksmanship principles - Overview

1. **Support & Position** - **The position must be comfortable and the hold firm enough to support the rifle**

- The chest must be as flat on the ground as possible.
- The left elbow is positioned almost immediately under the rifle.
- The left wrist is straight.
- The rifle rests across the palm of the hand, not base of fingers.
- The left hand is positioned at the point of balance of the rifle.
- The right elbow is positioned a little out from the body.
- If any form of support is used, it must be positioned to support the left wrist or forearm, NOT the back of the hand.

2. **Pointing (Natural Alignment)** - **The rifle must point naturally at the target without any physical effort or strain**

- The body is positioned to point naturally at the target.
- The shoulder and arm muscles must be relaxed, let the rifle point where it wants.
- To adjust the position up or down, move stomach and feet back or forward.
- To move rifle left or right, move feet and stomach right or left.
- Only minor positional adjustments are needed to acquire the correct alignment.

3. **Aiming (Sight Alignment)** - **The aim or sight alignment must be correct and the aim picture consistent**

- The head must be as upright as possible.
- Look through the centre of the rear sight, line up front sight with the target.
- Focus on the front sight, NOT the target (a sharply focused front sight and a slightly blurred target is expected).
- A sharp target with a blurred foresight is unacceptable.

4. **Release of Shot & Follow Through** - **The shot must be released and followed through without disturbing the position or aim**

- The first pressure (if applicable) is taken up while settling down.
- The trigger is squeezed GENTLY through the second pressure without 'pull' or 'tug'.
- 'Follow through' means that, when the bullet has fired, there is no further movement for a second or two.
- For a steady shot to be released, breathing must be controlled.

Aim

By the end of this chapter, you will have received the following lessons:

1. Introduction to first aid;
   The chain of survival
2. The conscious casualty
3. The unconscious casualty
4. Cardiac arrest
5. Suspected heart attack
6. Choking
7. Serious bleeding
8. Introduction to AEDs

Only instructors who hold an in date First Aid at Work or 18-hour Activity First aid qualification can deliver Basic First Aid and it must be delivered in accordance with the session plans found in the ACFA First Aid SharePoint (Heartstart resources).

If the course is being delivered through affiliation with a Heartstart or call Push Rescue scheme, the instructor must also have been assessed and approved by the scheme's Training Supervisor (at County level) to deliver the Heartstart course.

Instructors reference:

- First aid syllabus (AC 71101)
- The British Heart Foundation: The Heartstart Course
- St John ambulance first aid manual (revised 10th edition)

Introduction to first aid

First aid is one of the most important and relevant subjects you will learn in the cadets, as it is an important skill that can be used in every walk of life. Many cadets have been in public situations where their actions have saved lives.

First aid at a Basic level is designed to introduce you to first aid and how to deal with a life-threatening emergency.

First aid is the first life saving treatment given to a casualty

The aims of first aid are to carry out the 3 Ps:

- **P**reserve the casualty's life
- **P**revent worsening of the condition
- **P**romote the casualty's recovery

The chain of survival

This represents the sequence of actions that need to occur as quickly as possible in a life-threatening emergency.

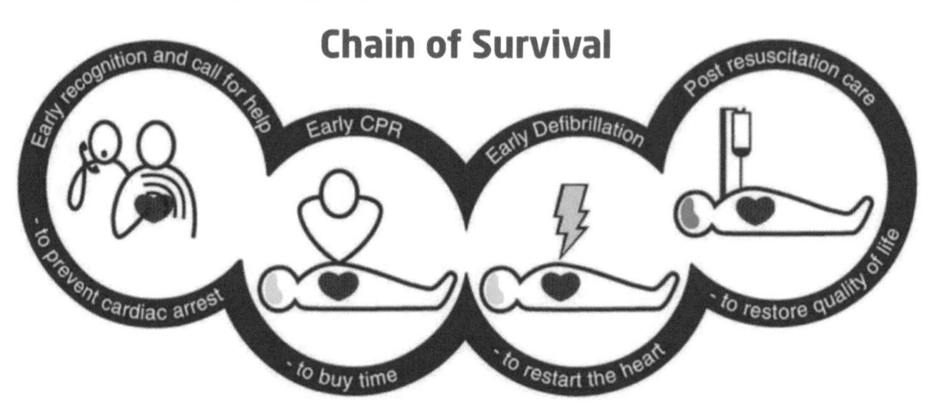

NOTE: You should not expect to see casualty recover spontaneously; the important thing is to buy time until professional help arrives.

Where is you detachment's first aid kit?

The conscious casualty

Primary survey (part one)

The primary survey involves doing a quick assessment of a casualty to see if any conditions or injuries are life threatening. The DRSABC sequence is carried out to achieve this, in this section we look at D and R.

D = DANGER

- Check you are safe and for any danger around the casualty.

R = RESPONSE

- Check for a response
- Approach feet first
- Ask a question loudly i.e. what's happened? Are you alright?
- Kneel down and gently tap their shoulders and give a command i.e. 'open your eyes if you can hear me'?
- There are 4 levels of responses: AVPU (Alert / Voice / Pain / Unresponsive)
- If the casualty responds by answering or moving, check their condition and call for help or 999/112. Leave casualty in the position found unless they are in further danger.
- After called 999/112 - continue to monitor casualty in case condition worsens.

Making a 999/112 call

Call the emergency services free on **999** or **112**. State which service you require:-

- Police
- Fire and rescue service
- Ambulance
- Mountain, moor and fell rescue
- Coastguard
- Mines rescue
- Cave rescue

The Ambulance Control Officer will ask a number of questions which may include some of the following, to assist it is useful to remember the word 'LIONEL'.

- **L** = Location
- **I** = Incident
- **O** = Other services required
- **N** = Number of casualties
- **E** = Extent of injuries
- **L** = Location (confirmation)

NOTE: Consider whether other forms of help may be needed and ask the Police to notify them i.e. Gas, Electricity, Rail, Water, Dentist, Midwife etc.

Casualty care

When dealing with casualties, remember the following:

- Be polite and friendly
- Ask permission to assist
- Always talk to the casualty, even if they are unconscious
- Listen and reassure
- Avoid cross contamination (use gloves &/or mask).

The unconscious casualty

Primary survey (part two)

On checking for a Response, if the casualty does not respond:-

S = SHOUT

- Shout for help three times if no-one is around.

NOTE: Call 999/112 only once opened airway and checked breathing:-

A = AIRWAY

Open the casualty's airway

- Tilt their head back
- Lift their chin

B = BREATHING

Check to see if the casualty is breathing

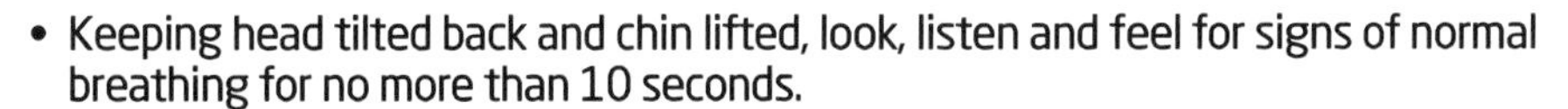

- Keeping head tilted back and chin lifted, look, listen and feel for signs of normal breathing for no more than 10 seconds.
- Agonal breathing - if you observe infrequent, noisy gasps this is not 'normal breathing'.

C = CPR or CIRCULATION

If the casualty is not breathing or not breathing normally call 999/112 and commence CPR. (CPR is covered in more detail on page)

If the casualty is breathing normally, then do a quick visual check for any signs of major bleeding, then put into the recovery position and call 999/112.

Secondary survey

This is done once all urgent life saving done and emergency aid given.

If the casualty is conscious, ask **AMPLE:**

- **A**llergies
- **M**edication
- **P**revious medical history
- **L**ast meal/drink
- **E**vent history

If they are unconscious (& conscious if the casualty agrees) do a top to toe check, ensuring you are wearing gloves. Remember to check for medical alerts.

Recovery position

If the casualty is breathing but unconscious, place them into the recovery position. This maintains an open airway so the casualty can breath.

1. Kneel beside the casualty (injured side). Remove bulky objects from pockets, and glasses or large rings

2. Place their nearest arm straight out

3. Make sure both legs are straight

4. Bring their furthest arm across their chest by holding the back of their hand against their cheek on your side. Keep hold of their hand

5. With your other hand, grasp their far leg just above the knee and pull it up, keeping their foot flat on the ground

6. Keeping their hand under their cheek, pull on their leg and roll the casualty towards you onto their side

7. Adjust their upper leg so their hip and knee is at a right angle

8. Tilt their head and chin back to open their airway

9. Monitor the casualty's breathing until the ambulance arrives.

Note: Do not put a casualty into the recovery position if you suspect a spinal injury.

Cardiac arrest

CPR (Cardiopulmonary Resuscitation) is used when a casualty has stopped breathing or has irregular (agonal) breathing.

After carrying out DRSABC:

C = CPR

If the casualty is not breathing or not breathing normally call 999/112 and commence CPR. If able, ask a bystander to call 999 and find an AED (see page 58 for further details on AEDs).

1. Put casualty on their back.
2. Give 30 chest compressions: Heel of hand in centre of chest / interlock fingers / keep arms straight / 5-6 cm deep at rate of 100-120 bpm (i.e. 30 compressions takes approx. 15-18 seconds).

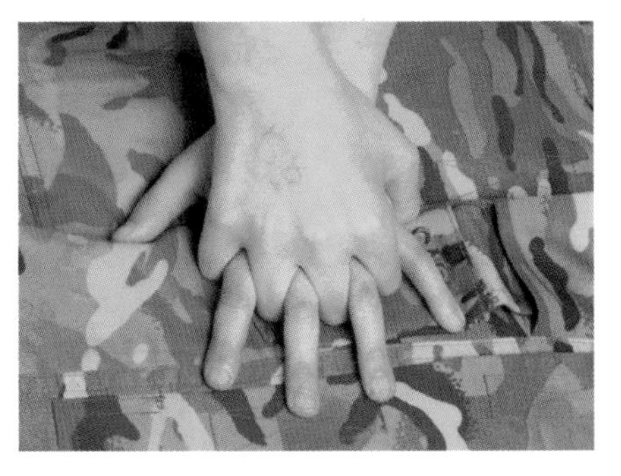

3. Give two rescue breaths (if feel comfortable doing so): Tilt head back, pinch nose and blow into mouth, watch to see chest fall. Do no more than two attempts.
4. Continue the cycle of 30:2 until either, professionals arrive and take over, the casualty starts breathing or you are too exhausted to continue.

Hands-only CPR:

If you are unable or unwilling to give rescue breaths, then give chest compressions only, it is certainly better than doing nothing.

Regurgitation during CPR:

The casualty's stomach contents may get regurgitated during CPR, if this happens, turn the casualty away from yourself onto their side to allow fluid to drain away, once done, commence CPR again asap.

Suspected heart attack

Signs and symptoms of someone having a suspected heart attack vary but can include:

- Chest pain which doesn't ease with rest (like a tight band wrapped around the chest) which can spread to one or both arms, back, neck or jaw.
- Pale and sweaty
- Breathless and anxious
- Feeling sick and may vomit
- They may become unconscious and have a cardiac arrest

Treatment:

- Call 999/112
- Get casualty to sit down, ideally leaning against a wall or something similar with legs bent (this reduces the work of the heart).
- Reassure and monitor the casualty until professional help arrives.

Introduction to AEDs

An AED (Automated External defibrillator) is a small lightweight 'shock box' that can restart the heart by giving an electric shock when a casualty is in cardiac arrest (heart has stopped pumping properly).

It analyses the casualty's heart rhythm and determines whether a shock is needed to restore the normal rhythm and pumping action of the heart to get the blood circulating again to get oxygen to the body's vital organs.

As part of 'The Chain of Survival' early defibrillation is vital.

Using AEDs:

AEDs are user-friendly devices that untrained bystanders can use. They can be found in many public places i.e. shopping centres, airports, schools. Turn on power button and follow the instructions:-

- Switch on AED
- Remove or cut through clothing on chest
- Take pads out, remove backing paper and attach to chest in positions indicated
- The AED will start analysing the heart rythym. Ensure no-one is touching the casualty
- Follow the voice &/or visual prompts given by the machine.

NOTE: Ensure casualty's chest is dry (and they are not lying in puddles of water) / remove any metal jewellery / do not place pads over implanted devices / remove any medication patches / do not use in a flammable atmosphere / shave casualty's chest if pads unable to stick to skin.

Choking

What you will see:

- Difficulty or unable to speak or breath
- Hands on throat or pointing to their throat
- Red-purple colour around neck and face with bulging eyes and a look of panic

What you should do:

1. Ask the casualty to 'nod if choking?'
2. Tell the casualty to try and cough
3. Give up to 5 back blows (sharp blow between shoulder blades with heel of your hand in an upwards motion)
4. Give up to 5 abdominal thrusts (arms around casualty, your clenched fist placed between navel and bottom of rib cage, pull sharply inwards and upwards)
5. Call 999/112 then repeat steps 3 & 4 until help arrives, obstruction clears or they become unresponsive. Always call 999/112 if you have done abdominal thrusts as they can cause injury.

Note: Remember to check the casualty's mouth after every back blow / abdominal thrust.

Choking infant (under one year old):

- Lay face down along your forearm and thigh and support head
- Give up to 5 back blows
- Using heel of your hand between infant's shoulder blades
- Turn infant over so face up along your leg and check mouth
- Give up to 5 chest thrusts
- Place 2 fingertips on lower half of breastbone and give 5 sharp downward thrusts.
- Call 999/112 and repeat above steps.

Serious bleeding

Recognition

- Bleeding wound
- Sweating and pale skin
- Breathless and anxious
- Dizziness

Treatment

- Check for danger
- Ask/assist casualty to sit down or lie down
- Ask casualty to put pressure on the wound and elevate limb if able
- Call 999/112
- Put on disposable gloves and assist applying pressure to the wound and bandage area if able.

Shock

- Shock can occur from trauma and blood loss, it is important to recognise and treat shock as it can lead to death if serious and untreated.
- **Signs of shock:**
  Blue lips, pale clammy skin, nausea, faint, disorientated.
- **Treatment:**
  Head down, legs up, reassure casualty and keep them warm.

Aim

By the end of this chapter, you will have received the following lesson:

1. Cadet in the community - Overview

Instructors reference:

- The cadet training manual (volume 1) - Chapter 10

Cadet in the Community - Overview

The Army Cadet Force is a voluntary organization sponsored by the Army and taking part in both military and community activities. Its purpose is to develop amongst its members the qualities of good citizenship.

Members of the armed forces have very varied roles, some of which are not of a military nature. Servicemen and women can be seen in the local community taking part in a whole array of different tasks, from attending parades and memorials to helping with major disasters and national events.

This approach extends out to the Army Cadet Force, and you will often see cadets helping in the local community by attending remembrance and armed forces day parades, selling poppies, helping maintain public monuments and attending fêtes etc.

It is important that when cadets are seen in public, they display extremely high standards of personal appearance and conduct. In some instances, cadets may be the only military representation at an event and should take extreme pride in wearing the uniform issued to them and show the utmost respect to the men and women that currently serve, have served or lost their lives in the armed forces.

Star level requirements:

- **Basic:** Overview of cadet in the community.
- **One star:** Overview of the emergency services and how to contact each of them. Assist in duties at your detachment.
- **Two star:** Visit one of the emergency services and provide a street plan of your local area with all emergency service locations marked. You will also need to take part in two local functions.
- **Three star:** Spend thirty hours over six months working on a community project, or a detachment project.
- **Four star:** Assist in the planning, organisation and leading of a three star project, or complete a study of the social welfare needs of the local community and provide at least thirty hours service over three months. Give a lecture to the detachment on decisions made.

CHAPTER TEN: Physical training

CHAPTER TEN

Aim

By the end of this chapter, you will have received the following lesson:

1. Introduction to physical training

You will also be required to partake in regular physical training and sports events at your detachment

Instructors reference:

- APC PT syllabus

Introduction to physical training

Fitness is an important part of army cadet training and helps prepare cadets for some of the strenuous activities they take part in. To ensure cadets are fit and strong enough to take part, certain standards are required at each star level.

Warming up and stretching

Before and after any physical training it is important to stretch and warm up.

Here are some stretches that can be done at any level.

NOTE: Do not attempt any stretches or exercises on your own until you have received proper instruction from an adult instructor.

1. Standing hamstring stretch

2. Single leg calf stretch

3. Standing Adductor stretch

4. Standing quadriceps stretch

5. Standing back stretch

6. Side stretch

Stretches (continued)

7. Standing chest stretch

8. Standing back stretch

9. Tricep stretch

10. Lateral shoulder stretch

11. Gluteal stretch (knee to chest)

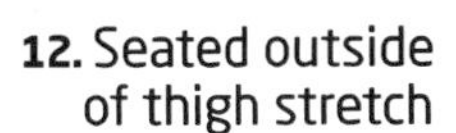

12. Seated outside of thigh stretch

13. Abdominal stretch

Press ups (hands and feet)

- Lie face down on the floor
- Hands under shoulders
- Palms flat on the floor

- Straighten arms, without locking, to lift body, leaving only palms and toes on the floor
- Lower to a position so that the arms are bent to approx. 90 degrees and there is a straight line across the elbows, upper arm and shoulders
- Return to the starting position and repeat the push-ups
- Scoring ceases if the body sags

- The score is the number of push-ups completed in one minute

Press up alternative (hands and knees)

Any cadets that struggle to complete full press ups as described above, can choose to do a slightly easier variation where the knees are in contact with the floor instead of the feet. Legs should be bent upwards.

Trunk curl

- Lie flat on the floor
- Knees bent between 70° - 110°
- Feet may be up to 10cm apart
- Arms folded across the chest
- Fingertips placed in the depression above the clavicle
- Elbows tucked into the chest

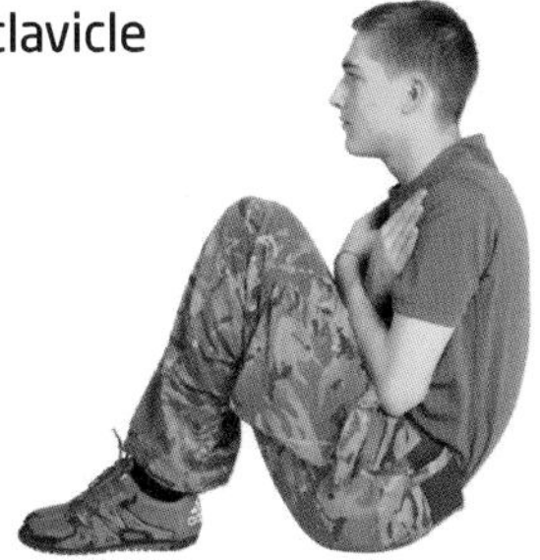

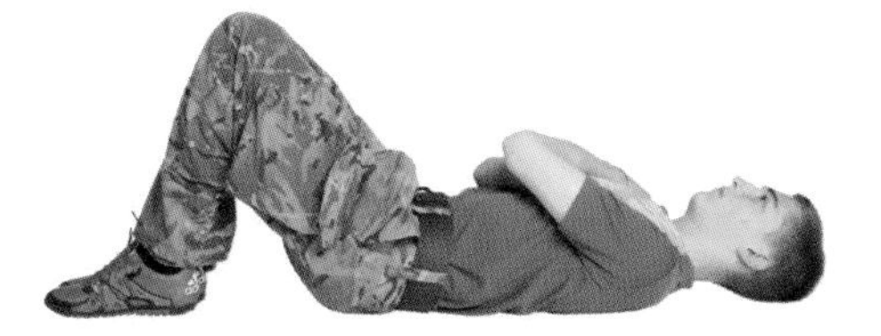

- Arms and fingertips must remain in this position throughout the test
- Curl up to reach the vertical position
- Then return to the Start Position
  (ensuring that the base of the shoulder-blades gently touch the floor)
- The score is the number of curls completed in one minute

Ball speed bounce

- Using a netball or size five football, stand behind a line two metres from a wall
- Hold the ball with two hands against the chest
- The ball must be thrown with two hands so that it rebounds from the wall into both hands behind the restraining line
- A brick wall or similar solid surface should be used to ensure a satisfactory rebound
- Scoring ceases if the ball is dropped or not thrown or caught with two hands
- The score is determined by the number of times the ball is successfully caught in thirty seconds

Bailey bridge

- Start in the front support position
  (Body in straight line supported by the hands and toes only)
- Shoulders near to and facing a chair on with a small object on
- Take the object from the chair seat with one hand, place it on the floor
- Pick up the object with the other hand and replace it on the chair
- Continue cycle

- Scoring ceases if the object is dropped or not placed under control
- The score is determined by the number of times the object is successfully placed on the chair in thirty seconds

Single leg squat

- Crouch with both hands placed flat on the floor and with the toes of both feet touching the front line
- Take one leg back so that the foot is on the floor behind the rear line
- Change legs so that each foot is alternatively thrust over the rear line, with the hips remaining high
- Scoring ceases if the feet do not cross the lines
- The score is determined by the number of single leg squats completed in thirty seconds

Run and sprint

The final two exercises that you will be tested on are the run and the sprint.

- **Run:** Run twenty laps of a rectangular circuit 12 metres by 8 metres (800 metres)
- **Sprint:** Sprint ten lengths of 9 metres (90 metres)
- Scores for these and all other exercises are in the final 'testing' chapter'

Aim

By the end of this chapter, you will have passed the following subjects and be ready to move onto one star training:

- Military knowledge
- Drill & turnout
- Fieldcraft & tactics
- Navigation
- Expedition
- Skill at arms
- Shooting
- First aid
- Cadet in the community
- Physical training

Military Knowledge

Cadet full name	
Detachment	
Company	
Date passed	

Score

Written assessment

A. History

1	When was the ACF first officially formed?
Answer:	
2	Who was the main founder of the ACF?
Answer:	

B. Detachment

1	Who is you detachment commander (DC)?
Answer:	
2	Where is the fire alarm meeting point?
Answer:	

C. Rank

1	Name one NCO rank
Answer:	
2	Name one officer rank
Answer:	

Pass: Get satisfactory responses to one question from each section

Assessors name	
Signature	
Pass or Fail	

Drill and turnout

Cadet full name	
Detachment	
Company	
Date passed	

Score

Written assessment

		Max. Mark	Pass Mark	Score
1	Name one aim and one purpose of drill			
Answer:		20	10	
2	Name two situations when you would salute			
Answer:		20	10	
3	Name one thing you should do to care for your uniform			
Answer:		10	5	

Practical assessment

Detail	Criteria	Max. Mark	Pass Mark	Score
1	Turnout	30	15	
2	Attention, stand at ease and stand easy	10	5	
3	Turnings at the halt	10	5	
4	Marching and halting in quick time	10	5	
5	Saluting to the front	10	5	
Totals		120	60	

Pass: Score a minimum of 60 points out of a maximum of 120

Assessors name	
Signature	
Pass or Fail	

Fieldcraft and tactics (No official testing requirements)

Cadet full name	
Detachment	
Company	
Date passed	

Score

Written assessment

1	What does CEFO stand for?
C.	
E.	
F.	
O.	

2	What does CEMO stand for?
C.	
E.	
M.	
O.	

3	Name one thing you would pack in your CEMO, but not in your CEFO
Answer:	

Pass: Four out of nine correct (not an official requirement)

Assessors name	
Signature	
Pass or Fail	

Navigation

Cadet full name	
Detachment	
Company	
Date passed	

Score

Practical assessment

Follow a given route in the local area, comprising of at least three legs that also include frequent changes in direction and covers 1.5 - 3km

Assessment date	
Location/route	
Length of route	

Detail	Criteria	Max. Mark	Pass Mark	Score
1	Identify and navigate using handrails	10	5	
2	The map should be orientated against handrails	10	5	
3	Maintain position on the map using handrails	10	5	
Totals		30	15	

Pass: Fifteen out of thirty correct

Assessors name	
Signature	
Pass or Fail	

Expedition

Cadet full name	
Detachment	
Company	
Date passed	

Score

Written assessment

A. Respect other countryside users

1	Name one thing that many would consider to be an intrusion on peace and quiet of the countryside?
Answer:	
2	What should you do with litter?
Answer:	

B. Respect those who work in the countryside

1	What should you not walk on when in the countryside?
Answer:	
2	What should you do with gates?
Answer:	

C. Protect the Countryside

1	1. List two ways you can protect the countryside?
Answer:	

Pass: Get satisfactory responses to one question from each section

Assessors name	
Signature	
Pass or Fail	

Skill at arms

Cadet full name	
Detachment	
Company	
Date passed	

Score

Practical assessment:

Weapon handling test - CSBTR

Test	Criteria	P/F
1	Order: "Take control of weapon"	
2	Order: "Strip the rifle for daily cleaning"	
	Question: . What size flannelette is used to clean the barrel?	
	Question: Show how you would remove fouling or debris from the chamber	
	Question: Show how you would examine the barrel for cleanliness	
3	Order: "Prone position down" then "Load"	
4	Order: : "Fire" then "Rifle fails to fire"	
	Order: "Rifle still will not fire"	
	Order: "Rifle fires alright" then "Stop"	
5	Order: : "Fire" then "Rifle fails to fire"	
	Order: "Rifle still will not fire"	
	Order "Obstruction failure to extract"	
	Order: "Chamber clear"	
	Order: "Rifle fires alright" then "Stop"	
6	Question: If after carrying out the IA twice the weapon still fails to fire, what should you do?	
7	Order: "Unload"	
	Order: " For inspection port arms" then "Clear, ease springs"	

Pass: No mistakes and questions correctly answered
Fail: More than one mistake, or any mistake that affects safety

Assessors name	
Signature	
Pass or Fail	

Shooting

Cadet full name	
Detachment	
Company	
Date passed	

Score

Practical assessment

- Two supported five round groupings practice shoot (minimum)
- Two supported five round groupings qualification shoot
- Practice shoot can be used if better than qualification shoot.

.22

25 metres

SCORING:

25mm = 25

50mm = 20

75mm = 15

100mm = 10

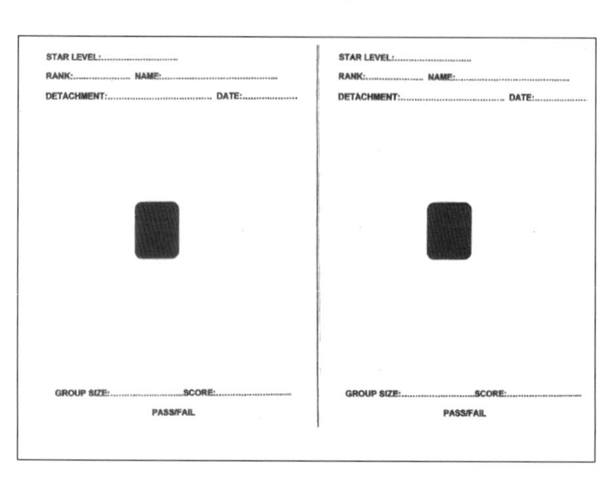
STAR LEVEL:..........
RANK:.......... NAME:..........
DETACHMENT:.......... DATE:..........
GROUP SIZE:..........SCORE:..........
PASS/FAIL

STAR LEVEL:..........
RANK:.......... NAME:..........
DETACHMENT:.......... DATE:..........
GROUP SIZE:..........SCORE:..........
PASS/FAIL

.177

5.5 metres

SCORING:

13mm = 25

19mm = 20

25mm = 15

32mm = 10

- Firing at targets similar to those above, fire five rounds at the left hand target and five rounds at the right hand target
- Aim at the bottom centre of the black rectangle
- You can rest your left forearm and hand on a support of some kind (sandbag etc.)
- Your score is based on the size of your group and NOT closeness to the rectangle
- The scores from both left and right targets are added together to get a total score.

Pass: 25 points out of a maximum of 50 points available

Assessors name	
Signature	
Pass or Fail	

First aid

Cadet full name	
Detachment	
Company	
Date passed	

Score

Practical assessment

Cadet to be given details of an accident and asked to contact the emergency services for help, they will be assessed upon whether correct details and location were passed on. (Example below can be changed).

A cadet at your detachment has cut themselves quite seriously on a broken piece of glass. They are conscious and breathing but are extremely anxious. You have been asked by your Detachment Commander to phone for an ambulance.

Using 'LIONEL' as a reminder, what would you say on the phone?

L.
I.
O.
N.
E.
L.

Pass: Result is pass or fail based on whether an effective message would result in the casualty receiving the appropriate help

Assessors name	
Signature	
Pass or Fail	

Cadet in the community (No official testing requirements)

Cadet full name	
Detachment	
Company	
Date passed	

Score

Practical assessment

Carry out activities at detachment or in the community

Date	Activity name and location	Hours spent	Witnessed by
	Total		

Pass: Perform a total of two hours helping with detachment or community activities (not an official requirement)

Assessors name	
Signature	
Pass or Fail	

Physical training

Cadet full name	
Detachment	
Company	
Date passed	

Score

Practical assessment.

- Complete four exercises from the list below
- Add the top three scores together to get PT test score (max available 15 points)
- Add up to an extra six points for detachment sports activities for overall score.

Exercises	Test	Gender	Points scored				
			1	2	3	4	5
Press up - Hand and foot **or** Press up - Hand and knee	Maximum in 1 minute	Male	15	23	27	34	50
		Female	8	14	18	24	30
	Maximum in 1 minute	Male	25	37	44	58	68
		Female	14	24	28	40	45
Trunk curl	Maximum in 1 minute	Male	20	28	34	40	45
		Female	10	20	28	32	36
Ball speed bounce	Maximum in 30 seconds	Male	30	35	40	45	50
		Female	20	26	32	36	38
Bailey Bridge	Maximum in 30 seconds	Male	12	17	19	21	22
		Female	12	16	18	20	22
Single leg squat	Maximum in 30 seconds	Male	40	60	70	76	82
		Female	35	50	65	72	80
Run 20 laps (12 x 8 circuit)	Best time (mins/secs)	Male	4.20	4.00	3.40	3.20	3.10
		Female	4.50	4.30	4.10	3.50	3.40
Sprint - 10 x 9 metres	Best time (seconds)	Male	28	26	25	24	23
		Female	32	28	27	27	25

Pass: 12 points
(minimum six from testing + maximum six from detachment activities)

Assessors name	
Signature	
Pass or Fail	

Lesson record

		Date	Instructor name	Signature
Introduction to the ACF	-			
History of the ACF	MK			
Ranks and badges of rank	MK			
Turnout - Care & cleaning of uniform	DT			
Aim & purpose of drill	DT			
Attention, at ease, stand easy	DT			
Turnings at the halt	DT			
Compliments	DT			
Saluting to the front	DT			
Introduction to marching	DT			
Marching and halting	DT			
Fieldcraft - Overview	FC			
Preparation and packing of equipment	FC			
Introduction to maps; care & use	NAV			
Intro to handrails & map orientation	NAV			
Handrails & maintaining position	NAV			
Expedition - Overview	EXP			
Using the countryside	EXP			
Introduction to shooting in the ACF	SAA			
Safety with weapons	SAA			
Rules for ranges	SAA			
Air rifle - Overview	SAA			
CSBTR - Overview	SAA			
Stripping, assembly, cleaning & maintenance	SAA			
Sight setting, safe handling of ammo. Load & unload	SAA			
Zeroing	SAA			
Marksmanship principles - Overview	SAA			
Introduction to first aid; The Chain of Survival	FA			
The conscious casualty	FA			
The unconscious casualty	FA			
Cardiac arrest	FA			
Suspected heart attack	FA			
Introduction to AEDs	FA			
Choking	FA			
Serious bleeding	FA			
Cadet in the community - Overview	CC			
Introduction to physical training	PT			